A SIMPLES LIFE

A Simples Life   Aleksandr Orlov

RUSSIA 2010

First published in 2010 by Ebury Press, an imprint of Ebury Publishing
A Random House Group company

Copyright © comparethemeerkat.com 2010

This is an advertisement feature on behalf of comparethemarket.com.
comparethemeerkat.com and comparethemarket.com are trading names of BISL Limited.

The Random House Group Limited Reg. No. 954009
Addresses for companies within the Random House Group
can be found at www.randomhouse.co.uk

A CIP catalogue record for this book is available from the British Library

The Random House Group Limited supports the Forest Stewardship Council® (FSC®),
the leading international forest certification organisation. All our titles that are printed on
Greenpeace approved FSC® certified paper carry the FSC® logo. Our paper procurement
policy can be found at www.randomhouse.co.uk/environment

Printed in China

This is a work of fiction. Names and characters are the product of the author's imagination
and any resemblance to actual persons, living or dead, is entirely coincidental.

ISBN 9780091944872

A SIMPLES LIFE

LIFE

MY LIFE & TIMES

by ALEKSANDR ORLOV

THE ORLOV FAMILY TREE

Aleksandr Orlov 1960

Anton Orlov 1906-1980 — **Valeria** 1916-1993

Anastasia 1867-1937 — **Grigory Orlov** 1871-1949 **Ivan Orlov** 1874-?

Nadia Orlov 1828-1892 **Tatiana Orlov** 1828-1891 **Vitaly Orlov** 1824-1879 — **Valentina** 1841-1898

Dmitri Orlov 1785-1854 — **Elena** 1797-1862

Katerina Orlov 1743-1801 **Isidor Orlov** 1741-1818 **Marina** 1755-1819

Kefentse Orlov 1698-1756 — **Kefilwe** 1703-1766

For Mama and Papa

CONTENTS

A MESSAGE FROM THE AUTHOR

MY name is Aleksandr Orlov. I live and make my work in Meer-kovo, small village outside Moscow. I have a success business. I have a mansion decorate with many fine things. I have a naturally majestic posture. But I would have none of these things if it were not for my family. I come from long line of the most courageousness, fearlessness, ambitiousness meerkats you could know. This book is dedicate to them.

In honour my ancestors, I also wish to inspire next generation of young businesskats. I am hope that this book will show what can come of courage, hard work and a good fur-care regime.

I am also hope that with royalties I will be able to re-marble roof on Orlov family mansion.

Special mention must go to Sergei, my head of IT. Without him this book would not have been written (because he record all my dictating on his cassette tape and spend all his holidays typing). Thank you, Sergei.

Aleksandr

K EFENTSE, as portrayed by extremely
handsome actor in epic movie,
The Journey of Courageousness. His faithful
companion is in the background, as normals.

PART *The* I

THE JOURNEY OF COURAGEOUSNESS

CHAPTER ^{The} I

In the Beginning

IN the beginning, my ancestors lived in Kalahari Desert in Africa. This is their story. It is full of endangerment and adventure, and complicated names, but I think you will be interest because it is, after all, where I am comings from.

It was good living in the desert. My ancestors built big burrows in the orange sand, and furnished them with characteristic meerkat tastefulness.

The days were long and hot. In mornings, when it was cooler, the meerkats would dig for grubs. In the afternoons, when it was hot and they were full of lunch, they would lie in the sun or take long, luxurious dust baths. (Just as I do now, although I prefer bubbles to dust.)

SOME Juicy Grub tins from the old days. They are empty, but if you lick the inside you ←❧ can still get the tangy taste of grub. And rust.

HERE is picture from movie where Seri is being bamboozled by empty tin. Sergei play this scene well, he is good at being bamboozled by everything.

On cold nights, the gang would gather round the fire and tell stories of courageousness. My ancestor, Kefentse Orlah and his loyal companion Seri (who was grey and bedraggly and full of fleas. Perhaps he remind you of someone?), were the most courageousness of them all. Kefentse would tell great stories of the dangers they had face. The meerpups would sit and listen with expression of wonderment. Seri would sit busy with his flea tweezers.

The only 'ointment in the flies' was the neighbouring tribe of mongooses. They were always sneak into meerkat burrows late in night and make thieves of themselves. Also, on windy days, their stinkiness would get in everyone's nostrils and make them feel sick.

But not including the mongooses, my ancestors lived happy

lives. Grubs were caught, and pups were born.

Sometimes, when Kefentse would return from a hunt (with Seri laden up with scorpion) he would invite meerkats from miles around to join their feast. They would come with warm worm puddings and bottles of beetle juice. Together they would roast scorpions on the fire as the meerpups played on their burrow sleighs.

On nights like this, Kefentse would look out across the plains and think: "Ours is a simples life. What could possibles go wrong?"

Then, one fateful day, disaster struck.

Having stirred from his burrow and done his sand bath exercises – sometimes his haunches could be stiffs in the morning - Kefentse went into the desert in search of fresh breakfast.

Two hours later he had found nothing. This was a bamboozlement and totally unexpectedness. He looked out over the plain. The green shrubs which were dot all over the desert sands

were now all grey and shrivelly.

It had been a hot summer. The air was dry and uncomfortabling. Kefentse had never known it to be like this. The hunger in his belly turned to worryness.

That night, the meerkats sat around the fire and had discussion. There was no food. A great famine had come to the land, and the landscape was getting dryer and dryer. The situation was absolute serious. Each burrow had enough tinned grubs to last a month or two, but after that…who could know?

Then one day, Kefentse awoke to an abominable discovery. Under cover of night-time, a mob of mongoose had crept into his

THIS is very old cave painting, as you can tell by how fadey it is. My ancestors would sit round fire singing the famous 'Scorpion Toasting Song' which has been hand down through many generation.

burrow and thieved the last of his tinned grubs. This was typical mongoosery, but it was still nasty shock.

Kefentse realised that he now had no choice but to leave to find foods. He had to find somewhere with wet rains and plants, somewhere with grubs and cockroaches where he could bring up pups and make a whole new life.

So Kefentse gathered all the belongings that Seri could carry and boarded up his burrow. The two brave meerkats said goodbye to their home and to their friends, waved a defiant two-claw salute in the direction of the stinky mongoose burrows and set off across the desert.

THE two intrepid adventurers were
scratched and tangled and weakened
by the sandstorms. And always with the
hunger grumbling at them.

THIS genuine real sand from Kalahari.
When I dip into jar with my claw, and
breathe the air I feel connection with my
ancestors and all they suffered. Sand also work
as excellent exfoliant.

CHAPTER The 2

Escape

THE meerkats walked for days and days. Between them they only had a few bags of beetle bits (plus not forget the fleas living in Seri's fur, but they would be last resort) and some precious gemstones of Seri's (which unfortunate were not edibles). The hunger grumble at them always. They invent new game, Eye Spy, to take their minds off it, but got stuck once they had done 'S' for 'Sand'. Mostly they just walk in silence, dreaming of caramelised larvae.

Some days the big orange sandstorms would sting their eyes and tangle up their fur. Other days, the quietness would boom in their ears and they would have to sing to keep from desert craziness.

"We are doomed. Are we doomed?" Kefentse would say.

"Yes, we are doomed." Seri would reply.

Then, one evening, after a long day's walk, Kefentse looked up to the sky and saw a cloud that looked like a meerkat's claw. Seri thought it looked more like a weird shoe, but Kefentse took it as a sign of good bodings.

THIS is exact model replica of 'The Courageousness', It took Sergei three weeks and approximate a million matchsticks to build.

Then everything in the distance got wobbly. Kefentse thought he might be seeing mirage. Seri thought he was having one of his funny turns. (He had delicate stomach, and often felt nauseous. Sergei like this, too. He often nause.) But as they got nearer, they see wobbly thing was the sea.

There seemed to be a small town near the shore. The meerkats hurried towards it, imagining all sorts of delightfulness. But when they got there it was very empty. Shack after shack was abandon. It was look like a ghost town in classic Wild West film (except they didn't know that, as films had not been invent yet).

Then they get to shack with a sign over it. It say 'The Queasy Mongoose Tavern'. Outside, an old muskrat suck on a clay pipe. They could smell his musk from where they stood.

The muskrat said he knew of beautiful far-off land full of grubs and beetles and grasshoppers. The land of Bermudas. He said he could sell them map and a boat to take them there. The meerkats thanked him and Seri generously donated his treasured collection of desert gemstones as payment.

The next morning they go to see the muskrat's ship. Kefentse thought it looked very 'rotty' with its sails full of hole and patch. But they took the map and with great courageousness stepped on board. Soon the ship, which they named 'The Courageousness', was full of sail. The meerkats looked at map. It was totally puzzlements, but soon Seri thought he had plotted course to Bermudas.

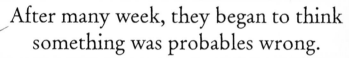

After many week, they began to think something was probables wrong.

After many week, they began to think something was probables wrong. It was getting very cold and still no land.

There were some old ship's biscuits in bottom of boat. Sometimes they found maggots in them, but mostly they were not that lucky. Seri often had one of his turns; he found the motion of the boat very upset and many time he had to pretend he search for meermaids as he lean over side of boat for hours. (This just like Sergei too. He bad sailor and have to lean over side of Orlov family yacht every time we go sail.)

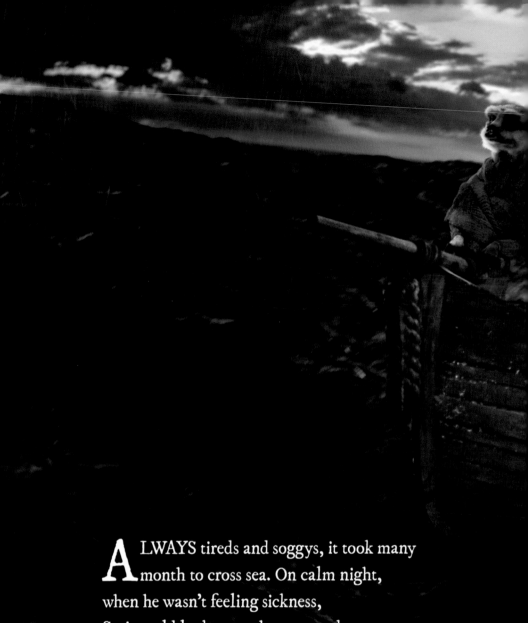

ALWAYS tireds and soggys, it took many month to cross sea. On calm night, when he wasn't feeling sickness, Seri would look up to the stars and imagine what worlds were there.

One Wednesday (they did not know which one) Kefentse was awoke by gigantic bang. There was huge ship with skull and crossbones waving at its mast, and mob of snarly creatures waving cutlasses on the decks. "Mongoose pirates", Kefentse thought. He had heard tell of these sea-faring mongooses. They would surely board 'The Courageousness'…and then who knows what? He might be kill, or worse, made to be mongoose slave.

MONGOOSE pirates have been romanticised in adventure books, but they are wicked creatures and not to be admired.

Just then, Seri poke his head up. On seeing his mangy frame and bleary eyes, the pirates went all quiet. Quick as flash, Kefentse shouted out that the mongooses could come aboard if they didn't mind about Seri's plague. With good timing, Seri made a disgustable splutter - this was really just down to his allergies but the mongoose pirates thought a terrible plague had infected 'The Courageousness'. They turned tail and fled away. And the meerkats lived to float another day.

One month later, after many more days of mumbling sea shanties and picking at splinters, they were still floating. And they still not know where they were.

Then one day there was crunching noise. They were going aground. It was end of the ocean! They climbed slowly out of boat and crawl up the shore....

Day 91 | Cloudy

I am think I have the scurvy.

My teeth feel wobbly and everything looks yellow.

Need fresh grubs.

Seri is shouting at the sea because he say it stole his dreams.

We must find land soon or we will surely eat each other.

Kefentse Orlah

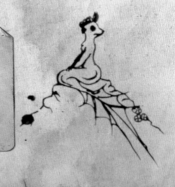

K EFENTSE kept a journal while he was at sea. It give shocksome insight into his fragile state of mind.

MY ancestors were happy to be standing on solidness after so long, but Russia was a long way from Bermudas, both in miles and pleasantness.

CHAPTER The 3

Russia

"**R**USSIA!?"
The word was echo around the big icy bay that 'The Courageousness' had landed in.

"Yes, Russia," Seri replied.

The map was mostly nonsense, but the sensible bits and the time they had been at sea made Seri conclude that they had landed in Russia. He was right.

Kefentse stood swaying in the wind. He was soggy and cold and

WHEN my ancestors arrive in Russia they were freeze, and after very hot Kalahari, they need to keep neck warm. This very first cravat made from scrap of sail. Later they were made of Pavlov Posid Russian silk. (Very expensive. I have 438 of them.)

very hungry. If he had given up it would have been understandables.

But Kefentse did not give up. He just tore a strip from the ship's sail and wrapped it round his neck for warm. Thus was the first ancestral cravat born. (And you thought it was just for stylishness.) Then he stiffened his bristles and set off into the shivery unknown.

He made it only nine steps into shivery unknown before giving up and collapsing on the soft, wet snow. Luckily, Seri (who was more energised thanks to his personal lice supplies) was able to drag Kefentse to the shelter of a cave on beach. There they rested. For next few days, Seri gathered what foods he could (mostly roots and the odd woodlouse) and Kefentse made battle with a frightful fever.

One time, Seri encounter family of marmots. He could not understand their language, but with paw gestures he asked for food. The marmots, being a kindful and generous species, were happy to assistance him and Seri returned to the cave carrying enormous bucket of millipede goulash.

(If ever there is a thing to revive a meerkat, it is millipede goulash. I have it still when I am struck with a touch of the poorlies. In a cave, in Russia, hundreds of year ago, Kefentse lapped it down hungrily.)

Three things happened over the next weeks. One: Kefentse

Map of the Krown World

Russia

Bermuda

Bermuda Octogon

slow worm gin smugglers pass

Africa

W E S

THIS is the nonsense map used
by my ancestors showing route
to Bermudas. Think of loss to Russia
if it had been accurates.

recovered his health fulsomely. Two: Seri built a fully-function flushing toilet in back of cave. Three: other meerkats started to appear on the shore.

It seemed that soon after Kefentse and Seri had left home in search of dinner, the rest of village had followed. They had track two sets of paw prints across desert and, in end, came across the muskrat from 'The Queasy Mongoose'. As he had done before, the devious muskrat pretended friendship and sold them nonsense maps and rotty boats. Months later, the meerkats begin to arrive in Russian bay, just as Kefentse and Seri had done.

If ever there is a thing to revive a meerkat, it is millipede goulash.

It was joyful reunion, but Kefentse knew their little cave could not support an entire village. So, Seri packed up his toilet and they all set off again.

They worked their way inland, across snowy mountains and through bubbly rivers. Graduals, they saw more green things, and discover tasty insects. Eventuals, they found a place that looked friendly and set up camp. First they build a cabin for Seri's toilet (it is said that this was first ever Russian public convenience) and then they made a proper village. They named it Meerkovo. And Kefentse Orlah of the Kalahari became Kefentse Orlov of Russia. And Seri became Seri Sergevinisky. And they both found lady meerkats to love, and soon the chattering of young meerpups was heard around their home.

Life was simples again.

THESE are snow shoes for separating the snow from the shoes. They are not actually the ones my ancestors used, but they could have been.

HERE is me in second epic movie. I was having bad fur day for this take, but we fixed in post-production.

PART *The* 2

THE BATTLE OF FEARLESSNESS

CHAPTER ^{The} 4
An Old Foe

TIME passed. And, eventually, so did Kefentse and Seri. Their sons and daughters grew and had sons and daughters of their own. Grubs were harvested and feasts were had. They had escaped the hardship of the Kalahari.

But they could not escape the mongoose.

Around the middle bit of the 1800s, nervous words spread across the land. A horde of Mongolian mongooses had been spotted swarming across the Russian steppes. These mongooses were bigger and worser than their African cousins. And their leader, Mongis Khan, was said to be the biggest and the worsest of them all. He stood at almost 5 feets, they said, and his claws were sharp as razor knives, and his stink…was unspeakable. He was determined on total conquerment and had, so far, stamped on any creature

A history picture of Mongis Khan, leader of the Mongolian mongooses. I think you agree, he look very pungent indeed.

Vitaly had flat paws so had to settle for the Meerkovo Home Guard.

who had stepped in his path. (All this is told in my Great Uncle Vassily's forty-one volume *History of the Mongoose Wars*. I have copy on audio-cassette, it make for many hundred hours of fascinating listening.)

At this time, the head of Orlov family was Kefentse's Great Grandson, Vitaly. (If you are paying attention, you know he is my Great Granddaddy, although he not know it yet.)

Vitaly was fearlessness. He would think nothings of taking on all a whole mob of mongooses with only a sickle and a hammer to defend himself with. Ever since a pup, he had dreamed to join the 5th Battalion of the Royal Meerkat Dragoon Guard, the most fearlessness battalion in all of the meerkat military. However, unfortunates, Vitaly had flat paws so did not pass physical examination and had to settle for the Meerkovo Home Guard.

THIS banner hangs on my wall at home. I have always try to live by the motto of the Meerkovo Home Guard.

MEERKOVO
HOME GUARD

PREPARE
FOR DINNER

CHAPTER The 5
The Battle

IT last days of autumn and the day before they were due to leave for battle. Captain Vitaly took his loyal Sergeant Serge out for one last beetle juice liqueur. Serge didn't really drink (it made him feel all peculiar), but he raised his glass bravely as his captain told him what was required of him on the battlefield: fresh scorpion on bed of parsley (served every morning in a silver platter), warm worm pudding and toasted cockroaches at snack times, and a fresh towel every day.

The Meerkovo Home Guard (who, as Vitaly explain patiently to Serge, were responsible for guarding the home part of the mountains) set off in good heart singing, 'They'll be coming round the mountain then they're doomed' at the tops of their voices. Soon they were setting up camps and Great Granddaddy Vitaly allocated sentry

THIS is actual horn blown by Mongolian mongoose soldier. Do not put your lips on it as you are likely catch diseases.

and soup-makings duties. He always made sure his troop had plenty of maggot and millipede soup. Because, as a famous general had once say: "An army marches on its stomach." Which actually sound very uncomfortables.

They then waited and watched for many weeks. Sharp-sighted infantrykats were posted on the high ground keeping their eyes out and their nostrils peeled for mongoose scouts. Once, young Private Potemkin had fallen asleep at his post (history say he had enjoy too many cockroach ciders the night before). He was reported for courts martialling, but instead Captain Vitaly put him on beetle-peeling duties for the rest of the war. (He was kind-hearted and mercifuls, my Great Granddaddy.)

Captain Vitaly rallied his meerkats. "Once more into your britches."

Early one morning, Vitaly was awaiting his breakfast. The snow was prickle his feets and his tail was awfully soggily. He sighed and watched his breath make weirdy creatures in the cold air.

Suddenly, Sergeant Serge appeared from behind a tent.

"Sir, mongoose army, in the valley," he gasped, clutching his telescopeamabob.

Somehow, a vast horde of mongooses had slipped through the front lines and was now marching on Meerkovo. At the head of them was none other than Mongis Khan himself. You could tell from the smell.

Captain Vitaly rallied his meerkats. "Once more into your britches," he cried, "stiff your haunches – do not let them smell your fear!"

The mongooses outnumbered the meerkats 20–1 and

out-stinked them at least 100–1, but the troops took heart from Vitaly's words. Sergeant Serge felt something stir in his haunches and decided it was courageousness. Together, they faced the mongoose charge.

The battle lasted through the night. From the rear, Vitaly managed genius defence. At the front, brave meerkats did deadly claw-to-claw combat with the terrible mongooses. Serge himself saw off fifty-seven of the creatures (and a small bush after temporarily losing his glasses). By morning, Mongis Khan had turned tail. The horde was defeat.

As the battlefield went quiet, Serge looked around and saw his Captain. Vitaly was lying on the ground, his blood staining the snow bright red.

Serge lifted him in his arms (this was not easy after all the toasted cockroaches Vitaly had been having). Cradling his friend and Captain, Serge let out a mighty wail.

This awoke Vitaly who was not dead but napping – it had been a long night. "Quiet down! It's just a fur wound," he said (in fact he had suffered minor accident with his scorpion-roasting fork). Serge wept with relief and said some things that he would later feel embarrassment about.

THIS is big rescue scene from end of *The Battle of Fearlessness*. Sergei is acting emotionals, and I am genuine worried he will drop me.

St.VLADIMIR

Soldier Hospital

PATIENT NAME: *Vitaly Orlov*

INJURY: *Scratch on haunch from scorpion-roasting fork.*

CONDITION: *Stable. Handsome.*

TREATMENT: *Ointment, fresh dressing, mild flirting.*

NURSE: *Valentina*

CHAPTER The 6

A Hero

IT was a giant-size victory for the Meerkovo Home Guard, but it had been hard won and there was lots of bloods. At camp, cheers of success was mix with groanings from the wounded. Vitaly agreed to seek treatment for his scratch at a soldier hospital in the woods. He allowed his loyal Sergeant to drag him there on a homemade sledge.

At the hospital, Vitaly was nursed by a very beautifuls nurse called Valentina. Day after day she bathed his wound with aphid oil and told him how brave she thought he was. They became intimateness.

One day a messenger arrived from the court of the Czar. As reward for his fearlessness, Czar Alexei the First (he was the ruler of

VITALY spent many week in St Vladimir Soldier Hospital. This chart reveal first hint of affections between him and my Great Grandmummy, Valentina.

all the Russias and very powerful) wished to present Vitaly with the Order of the Purple Claw, the most prestigious prize in Russia. He would also receive a great mansion-palace, built for him specials in his hometown.

Suddenly Vitaly felt much better.

He and Valentina and Sergeant Serge took the next convoy back to Meerkovo. There they discovered that the streets were full of cheering meerkats. They were overjoyousness at Vitaly's victory, and that the stinky mongooses had been routed and generally beaten about. Vitaly and his fiancée Valentina sat on their sledge, making waves to the crowds as Serge hauled them up the road to the mansion palace. (Many times I like to re-enact this scene with Sergei pulling sledge along very long drive at Orlov family mansion. Is tiring for Sergei, but I tell him he like to be part of history.)

> ## It was a day of magnificence and much feasting was done.

It was a day of magnificence and much feasting was done. Somewhere far away, Mongis Khan vowed to take revenge on the name Orlov.

THIS is detail from famous Order of the Purple Claw. Now it sits on my desk for inspire my Great Granddaddy's great-grandson Aleksandr, me.

PURPLE
CLAW

A hero image from the third and final film in the history trilogy. My Papa used to say his hat contain all his dreams, but really it contain snacks.

PART *The* 3

⟳

THE STREETS OF AMBITIOUSNESS

HERE is my Great Granddaddy looking most handsomeness on his wedding day. The family resemblance is much commented upon. This was taken on one of the first ever picture-majigs.

CHAPTER The 7
Hard Times

VITALY and Valentina's wedding was the talk of Meerkovo. A famous chef from Moscow created a delectable feast of three thousand roast scorpion à l'orange, four thousand millipede thermidor, two thousand ladybird soufflé and five thousand termite tarts. This was all wash down with eight hundred bottles of pricey Shiraz Scarab Beetle Juice Liqueurs. The guests make a lot of noise and dance through the night.

Afterwards, Vitaly and Valentina moved into new Orlov family mansion. It was very big and quickly became very full of fine furnitures (Valentina is no longer a nursekat, instead she is shoppingkat). For his walls, Vitaly commissioned many paintings of Orlov meerkats through the ages. These paintings become known as The Orlov Collection and are now famousness.

Before long, Valentina heard the clitter clatter of little paws. She and Vitaly were delight when she give birth to twin boy meerpups. They are call Ivan and Grigory and they have as joyfulsome puphood as any pup could wish for – how could they not with all the Orlov family mansion as their playground?

MY granddaddy Grigory and great
uncle Ivan with their mama Valentina.
This is last known photograph of Ivan before
his is disappear in disgrace.

Grigory was full of gratefulness and worked hard at school to make his parents proud.

Ivan was different story. He did not share his brother's sensibleness and would sneak out from school to visit the gambling dens of downtown Moscow. There he met seedy muskrats and played at cards with them. One day, after losing all his monies and both his boots, he bet the family mansion on his last claw of cards. He lost. (This is where the expression 'never play baccarat with a muskrat' is come from.)

Overnight the Orlovs became poverty stricken. Vitaly, Valentina and Grigory left the family mansion with only what they could carry in a small cart: the famous Purple Claw, two souvenir bottles of wedding beetle juice liqueur, some sea snake caviar and The Orlov Collection of meerkat paintings.

They had a very loud wedding that could be heard all the way in Moscow.

Ivan disappeared never to be seen of again. Some say he went about smuggling marmot pelts in Bulgaria. Others say he became a missionary monk and went off to convert the mongooses of Mongolia. Nobody know for sure.

Meanwhile, the rest of family set off to find somewhere to live. Vitaly had braved ferocious battles without wobble, but now he is frightened. Eventually they came upon a humble gypsy camp hidden in countryside. It was very different living from what Vitaly and Valentina and Grigory were use to, but beggars cannot be choosings. The gypsykats happily accepted them and the Orlovs settled into a simples life of grub farming, dung dealings and gypsy merriment around the fire.

One particular happiness was to come from this new life. While Grigory was out farming grubs, he met Anastasia, a glamoursome gypsykat. She was taking a dust bath when Grigory spied her through the bushes. He fall instantly heels over head in love. A few months later, Grigory asked her to marry him. He gave her a ring made of string and they had a very loud wedding that could be heard all the way in Moscow.

Soon Anastasia had a pup, and they call him Anton. (This, of course, is excite for he is to be my Papa Anton. But for the moment he is just small pup.) His grandparents, Vitaly and Valentina, were prouder than a punch, for Anton was very handsome and has strong haunches.

But this happiness was not last for long. In Moscow, a nasty faction of government meerkats had decide to rid the country of gypsy camps. The 'Furry Terror' swept through the countrysides. Simples, hardworking gypsykats were forced from their homes and sent to ghettos in the city.

Dreadfully, this was where my Great Granddaddy Vitaly and my Great Grandmummy Valentina met their ends. Grigory, Anastasia and little Anton wept for them in their tiny draughty apartment room.

The 'Furry Terror' swept through the countrysides.

CHAPTER The 8
Comparing Beginnings

LIFE in the ghetto was horribles, but Grigory and Anastasia worked hard to provide for Anton.

> Always he sat in back row of class and threw ink pellets at the swot-kats in front row.

They sent him to school where he studied English language and geography as well as Russian literature and mathematics. He was very talented (he is where I am comings from after all) but sometimes a bit lazy. Always he sat in back row of class and threw ink pellets at the swotkats in front row. One swotkat, who was called Stanislav, eventually asked Anton to make a deal. If he do Anton's homework,

> **T**HE ghettos were horrid, and a very different fish of kettles after the Orlov family mansion.

will Anton stop throwing things at him? My Papa thought this was fair deal and they became friends.

One day, Anton invite Stanislav back to his home. After they have had some ladybird tea and toasted maggots, they went exploring boxes. In one dusty box they discovered the many, many paintings of The Orlov Collection. Anton held them up for Stanislav (or Stan as Anton called him) and asked which one is better? Then it was Stan's turn. They were very entertaining themselves and went on comparing meerkats until it was dark.

Next day they skip school and spent whole day comparing. Then they did the same thing next day and the next day…and then they were caught. They were both put in detentions and told to write out 'Comparing meerkats is not clever and it is not funny' three hundred times. Grigory and Anastasia were furious.

But Anton was determined to prove there was something in his comparings, so one day in the middle of the night he fill his bag with all the paintings and ran away from home to make name for himself comparing meerkats in Moscow markets. Stanislav was left to break news to Grigory and Anastasia. They were double furious.

For support himself, Anton thought he would try entertaining. Performing in the middle of Red Square was magiciankat, the

Anton was determined to prove there was something in his comparings.

HERE is Papa Anton at height of his career. He has just land knockout blow on a mongoose.

Great Furdini. He did terrifying things like pretend to cutting up young meerkats and making them disappear. Anton offered to be his assistance, but after three nights of having his whiskers nicked by throwing knives, he retire. He decided to pursue less scary career and went to the Hotel Sovieto Splendido around the corner and got job as disher washer. In the evenings he practised his comparing which left him exhaust during day. Eventually he was caught falling asleep in the soapy water and given sack and thrown out into Red Square. Lying with his whiskers in the gutter, he felt sadder and more useless than he had ever felt sad and useless in all his whole life. But just by his nose was the foot of a big meerkat with bad breath. He drag Anton to his feets and tells him it is his lucky day. Anton not feel lucky, but big whiskery meerkat told him he going to make him a star. Anton, with no better thing to do, followed him down the steps to a dark and smelly cavern.

When he got there, he saw many meerkats in boxing rings, punching twenty-seven bells out of each other. It all look very violence. But the bad breath meerkat (who turned out to be Moscow's most ruthless boxing promoter) told Anton that he was purpose builts for boxing.

Before he knew it, Anton was getting ready for first fight – against Masher Egorov, the middleweight meerkat champion of Soviets. But not only did Anton avoid too much damage to his handsomeness, he knocked Masher clean out. This was beginning of Papa Anton's next job, as professional boxerkat.

It was a long way from his dream of professionally comparing meerkats but it kept the door from the wolf.

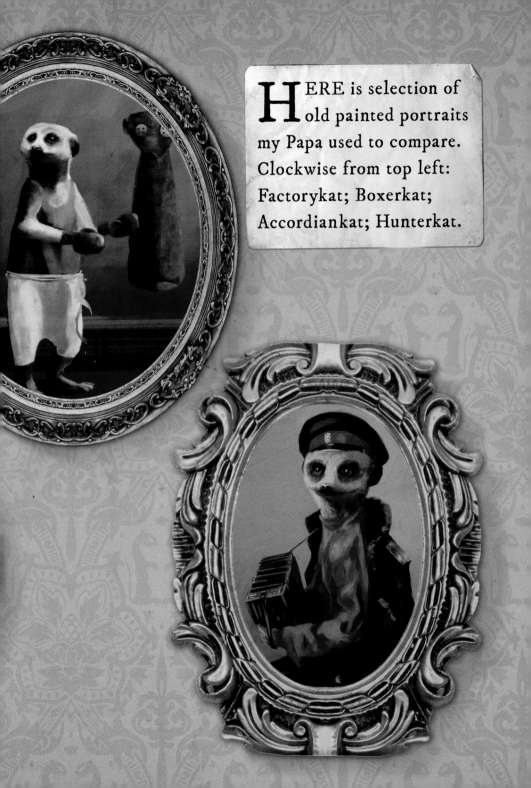

HERE is selection of old painted portraits my Papa used to compare. Clockwise from top left: Factorykat; Boxerkat; Accordiankat; Hunterkat.

CHAPTER The 9
The Shop at Last

BY now Anton was living in small bedsit and making a few more roubles because he was winning a lot of his boxings. It was hard work, and often he was bruised, but it was a living.

One day there was knock on bedsit door. When he opened it, he saw a familiar bedraggly face. It was Stanislav. He had now finish school and had come to join his friend. Good old faithful Stanislav.

Anton was very happy to see him, and together they decided that Anton must finish the boxings, and they must set out to make their fortune comparing meerkats.

The next morning they loaded an old cart with as many meerkat paintings as they could carry and made their way to Moscow flea market (which, puzzlingly and disappointingly, was not actually a market for flea selling). Anton neatly arranged the portraits of Knightkat and

Passer-bys could not work out what point of comparing meerkats was.

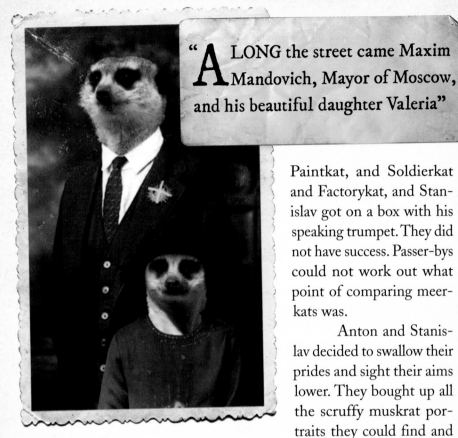

"**A**LONG the street came Maxim Mandovich, Mayor of Moscow, and his beautiful daughter Valeria"

Paintkat, and Soldierkat and Factorykat, and Stanislav got on a box with his speaking trumpet. They did not have success. Passer-bys could not work out what point of comparing meerkats was.

Anton and Stanislav decided to swallow their prides and sight their aims lower. They bought up all the scruffy muskrat portraits they could find and made their way to the seedy back alleys. Throughout the nights, they would let dirty old muskrats compare creepy muskrat paintings. It was shameful time.

During the days, they continued comparing meerkats in the market. They painted up the **compare**the**meerkat**.cart and made purchase of a little pointer for better comparing. But it was hard work. And for a long time no one was take much notice.

Then one day the crowds went quiet. Along the street came Maxim Mandovich, Mayor of Moscow, and his beautiful daughter Valeria. Anton looked at her and felt his insides go all wobbly. And when she stopped in front of the **compare**the**meerkat**.cart, he thought he might faint. Gesturing with a silk-gloved claw, Valeria told Anton to hold up Soldierkat and Knightkat, two of the most handsome meerkats.

Holding paintings in his shaky paws, Anton await Valeria's verdict. Imagine his astonish when she said, "The one in the middle." He was overcome with adorings. And this was the beginning of the big romance that led to my parents' marriedness.

After Valeria's comparing, my Papa's business went through the ceiling. Word of his comparings reached outside Moscow and the crowds came crowding in from miles around to see Anton and the faithful Stanislav compare meerkats. The two entrepreneurkats sold **compare**the**meerkat**.cart and bought the first **compare**the**meerkat**. shop. On the day it opened Anton's parents, Grigory and Anastasia, came to visit. Grigory shook his son's paw and Anastasia kissed him on the cheek. And my Papa got tears all over his new cravat.

MY Papa was force to compare muskrats in order to make meet ends. Do not judge on him too harshly.

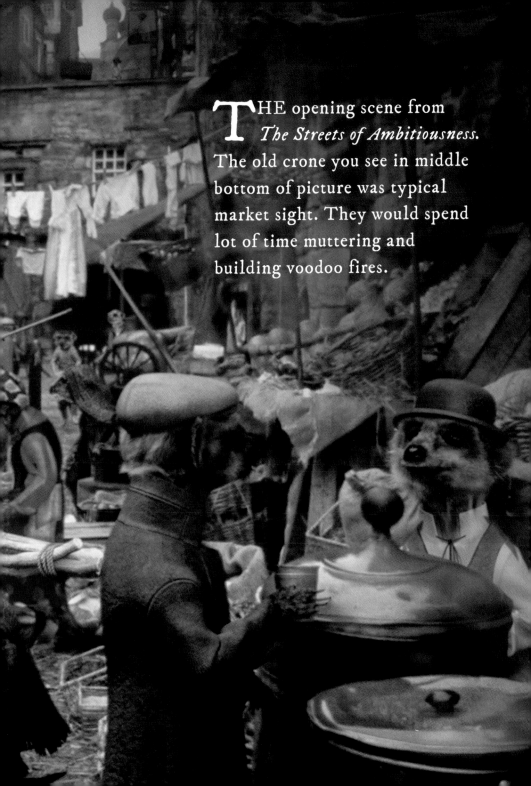

THE opening scene from *The Streets of Ambitiousness*. The old crone you see in middle bottom of picture was typical market sight. They would spend lot of time muttering and building voodoo fires.

H ERE I am looking magnificence in movie film *The Journey of Courageousness*. I kept the robes for use as pyjamas.

PART *The* 4

ME

F ROM early age I showed artist ability.
This is drawing I made of me with
my Mama and Papa at Red Square.

CHAPTER ^{The} 10

Early Days

THE night I am being born there was thunderings and lightnings in the sky. Was this because of warm front coming in from Ukraine? Or was it because the universe was sense something importants was occurring in the history of meerkats?

Whatever the case, I was for definites a specials pup. My Russian was fluented by age two and I could count up to a hundred grubs by age three. I had read *War and Peaces* by age seven and by nine I had written an epic novel entitle *The Enormous Adventures of Aleksandr the Adventurer*. My Mama and Papa were delight with little Aleksandr Orlov.

They sent me to school at Madame Meerstropovich's Academy for Talented Meerkats, which was full of the offsprings of the important families and was finest school in Russia. I was advance for my year and showed early sign of entrepreneuriousness with my 'Homework Done In Exchange For Tasty Food Things' business (it sound better in Russian). Very reasonable rates. 3 quadrilateral equations = 4 caramelised cockroaches;

2 geometry exercises = 10 sugared ants; essay on causes of the Meerkat/Mongoose wars = 1 scorpion. I think I am like the young Sugar Alan only nicer to look at.

At this time Papa was having great successes with meerkat comparing business. He had many shops (though he mostly work in flagship shop in Petrova Street) and once a month I was allowed to sit on counter and watch Papa do comparings. His loyal assistant Stanislav would teach me the comparisons, and I would hide his spectacles for pranks.

At school, I was showing skills for the amateur dramatics. When I was 15 year old, I made production of the play *Uncle Vanya* but with a car chase at the end which I wrote myself.

I was also talent at the sport. I learned the fencing, how to wield a golf stick, and to do the archery. I didn't take after my Papa and put on the box gloves because a lot of peoples say my snout is my best feature and it would be shame for damage it.

I made production of the play *Uncle Vanya* but with a car chase at the end which I wrote myself.

An Aleksandr Orlov Production

VANYA

The Play by Chekhov

13th September
Madame Meerstropovich Academy
Entry: 3 R

> Mongooses very fat and heavy, as well as smelly, so they go fast. But we are more nimbly, and we go faster!

But mostly I love the burrow-sleighing.

Burrow-sleighing start when meerkats live in burrows and not mansions. We sit on sleigh and zoom through tunnels at danger speeds. It is very excite and skilful and I was captain of our school team, the Meerstropovich Blurs (we are blur because we are so speed). We make mince-millipede of every other school in the district.

When I was last year of school, the Meerstropovich Blurs got to finals of Russian National Burrow Sleighing Championships. Very big day. We travel to Moscow to take on the Mongoose Sleighers.

Before we start I give the team a speech of rousingness, just like Great Granddaddy Vitaly had done all those years ago. "Stiff your haunches, put on your britches!" I cry. They all become very roused.

Was tense race. Mongooses very fat and heavy, as well as smelly, so they go fast. But we are more nimbly, and we go faster!

My Mama and Papa say they are never prouder than when Aleksandr win Burrow-Sleigh National Championships Trophy.

HERE I am cross the line in first place with my burrow-sleigh team 'The Blurs'. It was amaze feeling to have the wind in our fur and glory in our paw.

Forever Furry

(Andante)

Piano

Forever Furry, We are sure to be, Plainly you can see, ever furry,

Our nostrils keen and ears free of fleas Whiskers never tangled,

Forever Furry We are sure to be, Plainly you can see, ever furry.

Our haunches firm, we arise with ease Tails never dangle

down with mongooses

CHAPTER ^{The} II
Growing Up

EVERYONE know last day of school is emotionals. Very sad to sing the school song for last time (our school song, "Forever Furry", always leaves a tear in the eyes) and to say goodbye to people you will never see again until the Facebook is invented.

I had been very good during my schoolings but I am a little rebelling when I leave. Papa want me to go to the State University of Russia to study the Business Managements, but I am thinking that I would try my hand at singing. Everyone say my renditions of the song 'I Will Survive' is better than the Glorious Gaynor, plus I could do all the moves to the song Y.M.C.A, which is not as easy as it look.

THIS is school song. Madame Meerstropovich's Academy for Talented Meerkats was very big on fur care. School motto translate as 'Bravely and Furrily into the Future'.

> I have many idea for film, mostly they are about me.

Papa is understanding of this, and even buys me a very sharp white suit for help me conquer music world. He is best Papa a meerkat could imagine.

So with suit on and whiskers waxed, I went out for auditions. (Whisker waxing is not so populars now – like flare trousers and communism.) I would always sing same song: 'Are You Think I Am Sexy?' It was a big chart hit at the time and also very thought-provoking I thought.

However, I was not meet with success. Many record executives are not too smart and would not recognise an exciting mix of talents and sexiness if it came along and introduced itself politely. So I left frustratedly.

Next I went into the movie industry – I am great for producers because they get writer, director and star actor all in one packagement. I have many good idea for film but they are bit ahead of the times. (One of my ideas would later become main plot for *Back to the Future III*.)

To keep afloating I do works as 'extra'. (I can be seen for nearly six seconds in the final battle in *Nicholas and Anastasia Part 2*.) But it

THIS bring back fondful memories. I do not go to the reunions though because it make me feel old.

> I am successful moviekat actor, writer and director, and my snack breaks are as long as I want them.

did not make most of my talents.

Eventuals, I was sack as extra after striking for longer snack breaks. (They are laugh on other side of their cheeks now because I am successful moviekat actor, writer and director, and my snack breaks are as long as I want them.)

Then just as I think I will go into politics something terribles happened.

I got message that Papa is waking up with very bad headache. His headache got worse and worse and one day he collapse in middle of comparing Salonkat with Painterkat. The doctor was gloomy and say it all go back to his boxing days and there is not much he can do.

I go straight home and sit with my Papa. We talk all night about his life and told lots of rude jokes about mongooses.

By morning, it is all over. The curtain has come down on my Papa's life.

THIS is publicity shot I had done for promote my music career. I have 4,000 prints in box in attic.

Welcomes to the future

Compare the meerkat on Betamax!

Come down to comparethemeerkat.shop on Petrova Street to compare meerkats on all new Betamax teleprojectors.

Alternate, compare the meerkat from the comfort of your own chair with our exciting new mail order Betamax service.

See in shop for detail.

Aleksandr Orlov
Founder

- Front door delivery
- 14 day free trial
- Over 10,000 meerkats to compare
- Order now and receive two Bonus Kats
- **PIRACY** can result in up to 25 years in Gulag

Petrova Street

comparethemeerkat.shop™

CHAPTER ^{The}12

Success (and also Sergei)

AND so begin my commitment to the family business. After Papa's death I was very sad and spent much time comforting Mama Anton who is, obviousness, very distraughts. I promised her that I would knuckle up, put my ear to the grindstone and be the winner of bread. (I learnt my English well, so I had all the right expressions at the tip of my lips.)

With help from Papa's loyal assistant Stanislav, I learnt the business of meerkat comparison during the day, and went to business school in the night-times. It play havocs for my beauty sleeps.

When I was ready I made tour of all the **compare**the**meerkat**. shops in Moscow. I decide that business must be more twentieth-century, so I install hi-tech Betamax tele-projectors for better comparing. This was prove very popular for a little bit.

Soon Stanislav is ready for retire. He knew I needed some help

I put these press advertisements in local magazines. I am still backing Betamax.

SERGEI was award a medal for beating the NASAkats to moon landing. But they took it away when they find out he fake it up in his garage.

Ракетный дизайнер с медалью "Rocket Designer with Medal"

THIS is Russian Mir(kat) Space Program mug Sergei keeps on his desk. It is why his tea taste of sadness.

so he suggest I work with his nephew. Stanislav's nephew was Chief Designer of the Mir(kat) Space Program, but was having to leave his job because he fake a moon landing. So I invite him for chat.

One day, there was a knock on the bell. Full of shyness, a grey bespectacled meerkat walked into the shop. (I think you know who this is.)

Sergei introduced himself and we sat down to talk over a pepperfly tea. He told me all about his life which was not very interesting, but he also tell of new video inventions which would mean we could show comparing meerkats to people at home on their computermabobs.

This was very excite, and I could see new technology would invigorise my business. So I make momentous decision and ask Sergei to become my official Information Technology ('IT' for short) manager. I settle him down in small office at the back of the storeroom, buy him an enormous brand new computamabob with lots of buttons and a daisy-wheel printer and he is very thankful.

Some weeks later he has 'uploaded' three meerkats 'online'. When I look at screen I see vision of future. It is coming slowly, but it is the beginning of the business you know and love today.

HERE is Sergei and I on set while shooting *The Journey of Courageousness*. Sergei lost 3 claws in the 'clap-board' that day.

PART *The* 5

MY LIFE TODAY

CHAPTER The 13
Me on Screen

AFTER a few more month, Sergei has finished putting all the paintings on the computermabob. It is long process and often the servermabob breaks down.

But finally we are ready to 'launch' our 'website' on the 'internets'. Is all very excite when I press button for first time. Unfortunate, there was power cut at exact same moment, and we lost all the pictures. Sergei had to start all over again. It was very stressful for Sergei; he thinks this was when his problems with the worms start.

HERE is Sergei and I in our first advertisement together. He was moulting a lot from nervousness.

When we finally have lift-off (this is Sergei's space background speaking) it is as good as I had expect. The site is looking very professionals and soon we have many peoples coming to the site and say this is best meerkat comparing they have ever seen.

After a year or two we are totally dominate the market. Everyone agrees there is no competition. Then disaster struck. (Again.)

One day Sergei come into my office (where I am having relaxing whirly-bath) looking panty and full of sweat. It was not a pretty sight. He tell me that he is having interferences on our website with people who are asking questions about the sport-back coupés and the ten-year-old estates. This is dreadfuls. And puzzlings.

When I inspect screen in IT department it is true. There are all these mongoose brains who are confusing '**compare**the**meerkat**.com' with '**compare**the**market**.com'. This is terrible threat to my business. And terrible insult to my ancestors.

So I decide that I must teach these mongoose brains out there to know the difference between the two. They don't even sound the same! (And that becomes one of my first messages on the televisionmabob.)

S ERGEI is in love with computermabobs. This one is vintage Soviet.

THE BATTLE OF FEARLESSNESS

AN ALEKSANDR ORLOV PRODUCTION
STARRING ALEKSANDR ORLOV

NOT SUITABLE FOR MONGOOSES
May contain scenes of extreme heroism

COMING APRIL 2010

ALEKSANDR ORLOV PRESENTS IN ASSOCIATION WITH MEERMAX 'THE BATTLE OF FEARLESSNESS'
ALEKSANDR ORLOV WITH SERGEI CASTING BY ALEKSANDR ORLOV
EDITED BY SERGEI PRODUCED, WRITTEN AND DIRECTED BY ALEKSANDR ORLOV

MEERMAX

CHAPTER The 14
Making of the Movies

EVEN though I have many educational advertisements on television, some peoples still confused. That is why I decided to up the ants and make thrilling and tender sixty-second epic movie films of my ancestors' story: the courageousness journey from Kalahari to Russia; the fearlessness battle against evil mongooses; and the ambitiousness building of a business empire. You have already been amazed by shots from these movie films in first half of this book.

Casting for films was simples. Obviously there was only one meerkat who could play leading role (and it was not going to be Sergei!). I do not want toot my horn, but I think I have set new standard of acting and should have clean sweep at the Oskats next year.

For director, I chose myself also. Telling peoples what to do is one of my favourite hobbies, so job come naturals.

> Telling peoples what to do is one of my favourite hobbies, so job come naturals.

I was fortunate to work with such a talented actor as myself, but directing Sergei was like trying to direct a blob of cheese. He is good at computermabob, but cannot act his way out of paper hat.

In first film, *The Journey of Courageousness*, we film escape from Kalahari Desert. I am method actor, so to get into character for desert scene I practise by lying on beach.

When we were on location in Kalahari, limo would often get stuck in sand dune and Sergei would have to dig out. He said I should never have brought limo to desert in first place, but where else was I supposed to chill my beetle juice liqueur?

Many peoples ask me what is my favourite film. Is easy: *Titanic*, because it is best film ever made. My favourite line in movie is: "Jack, I want you to draw me like one of your French girls" because there is lot of subtext in that. Also I love the bit where Jack and Rose are stand at front of boat and he is spread his arm wide and it is like they fly across ocean on wings of love. I try to re-enact scene with Sergei when I film dramatic ocean sequence in *Journey of Courageousness*, but he was not keen to do it.

Second part of Orlov Family History Trilogy is *The Battle of Fearlessness*. It tell story of my Great Granddaddy Vitaly's victory over the Mongolian mongoose, Mongis Khan.

Film was shot on actual site of battle in the Ural Mountains and features genuine replica uniforms and flags paw-sewn by Sergei. I star as Great Granddaddy Captain Vitaly and Sergei plays his loyal Sergeant.

I created these storyboards for help with filming *The Journey of Courageousness*. Each frame took three days to draw. ✍➤

5. Hero Shot

Exterior c/u: Kefentse doing
expert flouncing

6. Kefentse & Seri on dune

Enter Seri with grub

7. Grub Tin

Cut to Seri looking at empty grub
tin with hungry look in his nose

8. Desert

Cut to wide. Kefentse and Seri
look like tasty little ants in
middle of big desert

9. Kefentse on boat

Cut to c/u. Kefentse battles
the topsy-turvy sea

10. Seri on boat

Cut to c/u. Seri battles his
topsy-turvy belly

11. Landing in Russia

Cut to c/u. Kefentse collapsed,
but handsome

12. Kefenste & Seri on snow

Cut to mid-shot. SMASH ZOOM OUT!

Supporting cast includes brigade of brave meerkat soldiers who I borrow from local burrow and horde of authentic mongooses who I find skulking around bins behind 24-hour grub store. For my fur wound, Sergei make very realistic bloods with tomato sauce, which I later used in sandwich.

For Part the Three we are in Moscow with *The Streets of Ambitiousness*. Here we are see the beginning of the Orlov family business empire. We film on Petrova Street – originals site of first **compare**the**meerkat**.shop, but we make it look like it is long time ago using costumes and mud.

For role of mischievous Urchinkat twins we cast actual pair of mischievous Urchinkat twins. I think they will go on to be famousness with this incredibles start to their career.

I great enjoyed the process of movie making and, who know, when I have finally compare my last meerkat, maybe I will have career in Holly Woods. Not as glamorous as compare meerkats, but I would like to conquer rest of world with my actings, and put my star on the pavement.

PS: When they make movie of my life, I would like Emilio Estevez play me, and Danny DeVito play Sergei. There is no negotiation on this.

> I managed to write, act, direct, produce and get spa treatment all at same time. Sometimes I am amazing myself.

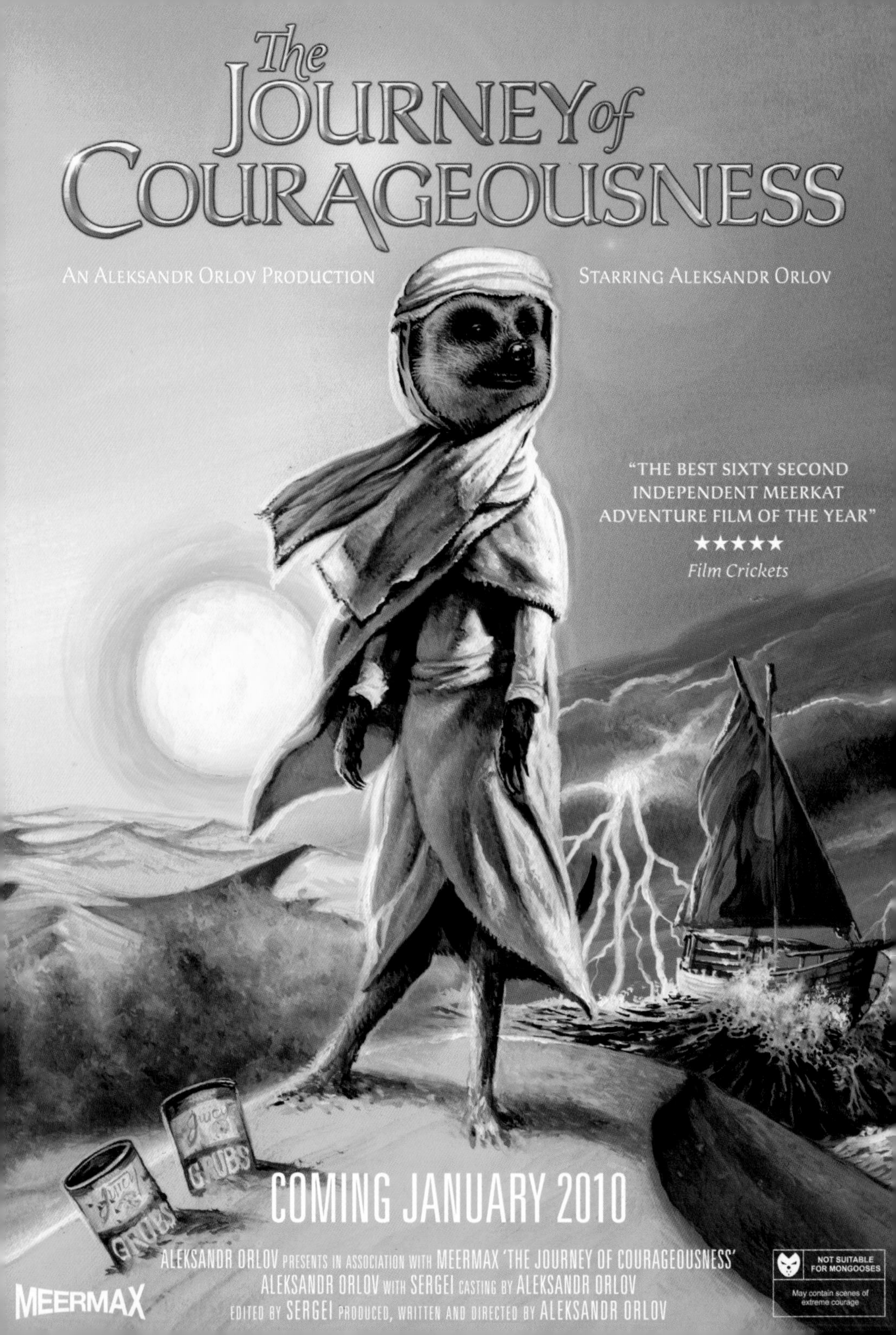

CHAPTER The 15
At Home

ORLOV Family Mansion is many years ancient. But, as you remember, Great Uncle Ivan had lost it in game of baccarat and it became home to a pack of dirty muskrats. Fortunates, with my new wealthiness, I was able to buy it back and restore family honour. I also restore the carpets which were filthy.

When it was mended, it was very excite day to enter the mansion for the first time. Right away I sent Sergei into attic for explore. It was trove of treasures. Sergei found: a box of fossilised scorpions, some mongoose fur slippers, my Great Granddaddy Vitaly's battle fork, an old rocking wolf, a beautiful puppet theatre (complete with puppet

HERE is me on one of the grand staircases. Banisters are 405 feet long top to bottom. If properly varnish, I can slide whole thing in 17 seconds.

people), a genuine antiquey Fabergé omelette and a family of sparrows who attacked Sergei with their beaks. He also discover world's largest collection of balalaikas, which my Great Uncle Ivan used to play loud after comparing beetle juice liqueurs. Sergei spent many hours dusting and cataloguing these treasures. It was messy business as treasures were cover in dust and old fleas, but at least that make him feel at home.

Mansion Facts

◆ My home is a bit like English palace of Bucking Hams, only bigger. There are 58 staircases with 3,460 stairs and I estimate about one million door knobs.

◆ Every spring Sergei does the clean. It is no park walk. He gets through 5 mops, 12 brooms, 16 dusters, 4 vacuum cleaners and 6 box of dust allergy medicine.

◆ Quad is big enough for Moscow State Circus to do whole show. Best part is the trapeze swings, closely follow by the cannonball swallower.

◆ My cinema has its own reclining throne and popcockroach maker.

◆ My wardrobe is made from expensive wood. It contains many cravats made of purest silk from free-range silkworms. I also have some spun by specials Croatian glow-worms so I can find way to toilet at night.

◆ I own a falcon called Dmitri who nests in a dome on roof. He is well trained and can spot a mongoose at 1000 yard. (So, if you are mongoose, and you are read this in order make burglary, you have been warn.)

◆ Telescopeamabob in rooftop observatory can spy on all the planets. Sometimes I let Sergei use it for relive the old days.

NURSERY is home to my puppet theatre. I am master of the puppets and perform several award-winning productions here, including Antigone and *2 Fast 2 Furious*.

FLOOR PLAN
ORLOV MANSION

1. **Office**
Sometimes I am spend almost
four hour at a time here.

2. **I.T. Dept**
Sergei's home from home.

3. **Stationery Cupboard**
Sergei's holiday home from home.

4. **Mirror Maze**
Sometimes I get lost
in my own stylishness.

5. **Drawing Room**
I also use this as Archery Range.

6. **Corridor**
Doubles as Skittles Alley.

7. **Cinema/Theatre
/Karaoke Room**
Sometimes all at once.

8. ~~Secret Room~~

9. **Gymnasium**
Where I perform gruelly
daily haunch exercises.

10. **Wardrobe** (level 1)
Contains 3,679 different type of cravat.

11. **Bath Spa**
Houses Olympics-size tub and wave machine.

12. **Golf Corridor**
I have already destroy
three granddaddy clocks.

13. **Old Nursery**
Makes me feel like a meerpup again.

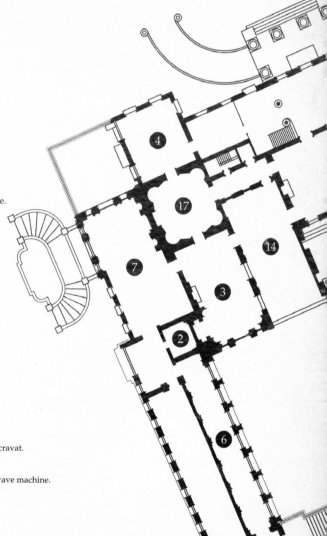

14 **Library**
Contains over 60,000 books and 11 secret passages.

15 **Ballroom**
And Balloon Room on Saint Vladimir's Tuesday.

16 **Real Vault**
Includes World's only Fabergé Omelette.

17 **Fake Vault**
Includes World's only fake Fabergé Omelette.

18 **Banquet Hall**
This is where I while away the afternoon.

19 **Grub Pantry**
Sergei is always sneak caterpillar crepes from here.

20 **Kitchen**
The birthplace of Sergei's famous beetle broth.

21 **Tunnel Entrance**
I burrowed from this end.

22 **Panic Room**
For when I am in a panic.

Sergei's House Where Sergei does what

Gate House
Where I keep
my collection of gates.

Stables
I like to race horses,
but they are always beat me.

Orlov Mansion

Aviary
Where I keep my
loyal falcon 'Dimitr

Lake
Where I have my
early morning swim
once every ten years.

As you see from plan, I have big grounds. We used to have hedge maze based on Cretan Labyrinth at Knossos, but one time Sergei was on way home from working in mansion and lose himself in maze for three days. He was found by gardeners covered in hedge mites. We got rid of maze after that.

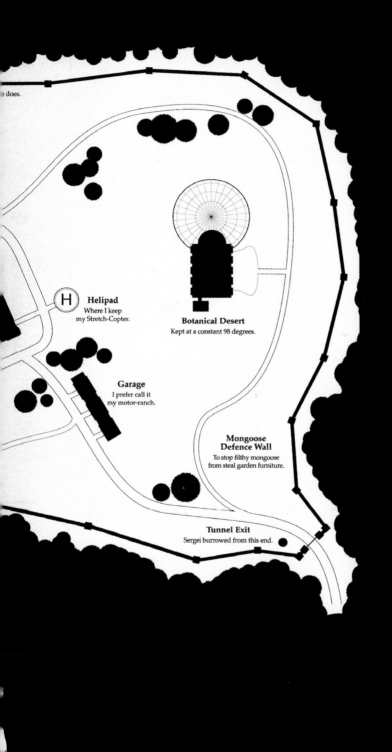

does.

Helipad
Where I keep
my Stretch-Copter.

Botanical Desert
Kept at a constant 98 degrees.

Garage
I prefer call it
my motor-ranch.

**Mongoose
Defence Wall**
To stop filthy mongoose
from steal garden furniture.

Tunnel Exit
Sergei burrowed from this end.

MY bathroom is newly refurbed with an Olympics-size swimming pool for my exercisings. My record is 21 lengths (any thing more than that I get cramp in my tail). Is much more tiring than compare meerkats.

Afterwards I have soothing whirly-bath. Sometimes bubbles is not work though because Sergei's fur moultings is block the bubble pipe. Then we have to call out plumberkat and Sergei hides in his room because he is embarrassment.

Eats

I do not actually do cookings (Sergei wears the chef
hat in this house) but I know all about good foods.
Eating is probables my third favourite hobby
behind meerkat comparing and cravat collecting.
Here is some menu ideas for you.

Menu ideas for you

The Breakfast

My Papa say tasty breakfast is foundation of tasty day. I like to wake
up to 8 scorpion sausage, 3 egg, 4 termite toasties with fruitfly jam
(or organic centipede and maggot marmalade if I am feel tangy)
and a bowl of Beetlebix.

The Lunch

Dustmite appetiser, then roast scorpion with cranberry and beetle
stuffing is very good. For simpler occasions scarab beetle burger
with cheese and mushy fleas is good. Except mushy fleas
go straight to the hind.

The Picnics

Gekko sandwich with extra millipede mustard.
Stag beetle and cheese panini.
Centipede baguette with mayfly mustard
(but not too much with the mustards as it is make me windy).

The Tea

In afternoons, I like sit in drawing room toasting maggot muffins in
front of fire. Or eating digestives biscuits, dunked in
pepperfly or ladybird tea. And then a snooze.

The Dinner

For starter I like chilli grasshopper legs (they have quite a kick)
or dung beetle salami.

Then for the big course, one of my favourite
is roast scarab beetle with mini cabbage and grub gravy.
(Never brussel sprout though - they taste like the back of Sergei's
watch strap). Or I have millipede thermidor then scorpion a l'orange
(just like my Great Grandmummy Valentina cooked it).

For pudding I like banana with drizzle of cockroach custard or
double maggot cream. In winter, sometimes Sergei is allowed
into dining room for takeaways and Battleships game evening.
I have Fire Ant Masala, and he have Creamy Cricket Korma.
(He always try to win at the Battleships, but he has no hope.
I once sink 40 ship at once with remote control bomb plane.
Not good night for Sergei.)

Here I am with my vintage Rolls-Royce before we go for picnic. Sergei very good driver – he can make drive from mansion to front gate in only 25 minutes now.

I have many rooms for sport in my home; here is drawing-room archery. This is where I successfuls shoot a fruit off top of Sergei's head on only third attempt.

THE END

CONGRATULATION! You have reach the end of my book. I am hope you have enjoy reading it as much as I enjoyed dictating it.

If you are take just one thing from this book, it should be that meerkats are an amazing and diverse species. From brave hero meerkats like my Great Granddaddy Vitaly to nervous computery meerkats like Sergei, we are all unique – like snowflakes or batteries in my closet.

Thank you.
Sincerity,

Aleksandr

PS: Sometimes it can be a bit sad to reach end of a really fantastic book, so for specials treat I have include some of my favourite **compare**the**meerkat**.com meerkats in dedicated appendix. You are welcomes.

APPENDIX

A Selection of comparethemeerkat.com Meerkats

KENDOKAT *Miami*

Kendokat wields big stick and wears specials designed armour. He look scary but actually is very nice. When not engaging in extreme combat, Kendokat likes picnicking and pedalling boats shaped like swan.

This meerkat can often be found on Miami Beach perfecting squat thrust technique or discussing sunglasses straps with training partner.

BIKERKAT *Honolulu*

Get your motor running, head out on the highway, Bikerkat is oiled up and ready to ride. Liking nothing better than wind in whiskers and hot tarmac under wheels, Bikerkat once rode 700 miles just to get a burrito.

On lazy days this meerkat love sit under shade of palm tree knitting grass skirt and flower necklace in readiness for night-time beach Lu'au. During the week he runs a shack selling exotic seashells and boogie boards to tourists.

BALLETKAT *Weston-super-Mare*

Balletkat is little clumsy round the house but when on stage and in tutu, there is transform into most graceful and elegant creature. Very flexible and able to leap large distances – useful when queuing.

This meerkat goes to Weston-super-Mare to play slot machine and snog stranger outside closed beach bar or stand in middle of gigantic empty car park when feeling sickness of home in Kalahari.

PARTYKAT *Bangkok*

A 24-hour party animal. If there's a dance club having a massive dance party, Partykat is surely going to be there with glow sticks, disco pants and spirit of sexiness.

This meerkat love spiritualism of Bangkok dance scene and has taken 'sacred vow of the boogie'. Now committed to new life of throwing shapes in golden temple of dance.

POSTSCRIPT FROM SERGEI

THIS has been very tiring exercise. Plus it has used up all my typewriter ribbons. Worst bit was when pages blew away in wind and I had to start all over again. I hope that – *Note from Author: Sergei, we have limit space so I will have to stop you there. Apologies. Also, my computermabob will not switch on. Can you have a look?*

"You've read the bookamabob, now listen the audiomajig!"

Read by Aleksandr Orlov

Available to download from iTunes or www.audible.co.uk/simples